T0365333

The
Goddess Wheel

A Meditation Guide on Woman's Sacred Cycles and Sexual Mysteries

Karin E. Weiss, Ph.D.

To order additional copies of this book, contact:
Xlibris
1-888-795-4274
www.Xlibris.com
Orders@Xlibris.com

A Sacred Wheel of 8 Feminine Archetypes

The moon is the mirror
of the Goddess.
It reflects her variable faces
in its transitory phases.
Women watch the changing
faces of Goddess to
reflect on our own
many-faceted selves.

Feminine spirituality is about becoming Whole.
It is about containing, connecting, uniting, and bonding.
It is about affirming and celebrating all living things.
It is about harmonizing and balancing the masculine and
feminine principles in all our lives.

The Mother-god's most important lesson is that
Divinity exists in everything; that all life is sacred and
erotic. Her lessons are shown in circles, cycles, spirals,
webs, and wheels— symbols of turning, holding, enfolding,
embracing, and returning— which are all metaphors for life
in the feminine way.

The feminine spiritual message is perpetually
revealed by the turning of the seasons, and, above all,
we see our own experience of transitions and changes
mimed by the moon's monthly orbit. Like the "faces"
of the moon, women's own cycles, moods, and roles
pantomime the ever-changing Essence of female sexual
and spiritual power.

NEW MOON
WINTER SOLSTICE

A New Moon is a symbol of conception, of containment, of waiting, of gestation, of bringing forth, and of release. As the moon orbits between earth and sun, it becomes completely encircled by the sun's aura, embraced in the sun's light. Just so, it can be a sign of how life begins with the merging of sperm and egg; of how the embryo is embraced, contained in the mother's womb; of how a seed is held, nourished, in the soil of earth; of how a new idea is conceived and gestates in our mind.

NEW MOON
Kanu Weiss
2/2003

WINTER SOLSTICE:
(December 21)
Longest Night.
Ancient goddess cultures understood that these Dark Times were times of endings and new beginnings. They were times of prophecy and of waiting for something to happen; watching for something to come out of hiding. Light increases. The newly born emerges.

CRESCENT MOON
CANDLEMAS

Following the period of New Moon darkness, a shy smile of moon appears near the western horizon at sunset. Still hidden within Earth's shadow, the moon at this stage presents a fleeting, tantalizing vision. It represents a phase of instinctive, youthful, unconscious, and irrepressible activity. Thus, it corresponds to the Maiden's passage in our lives— a time of self-determined realities, untouched by worldly limits, filled with potentialities as yet uncorrupted by society's conventional judgments.

IMBOLC:
(February 1)
Winter's end. Traditionally, this is a time of purification and prophecy, observed by the lighting of candles to spark new growth. A debut, a time of "coming out" and a focus on instinctive creative activity, it is marked by festivities dedicated to virgin goddesses in many parts of the world. The lighting of candles honor an innocent, instinctive joy in simply being alive and awake.

FIRST-QUARTER MOON
SPRING EQUINOX

The waxing half-moon rises around noon, and hovers, translucent, in a clear daylight sky. Then, it pierces the night with its half-light, until setting shortly after midnight. Its shape suggests something of an opened cocoon, or a broken egg— something released from containment. Like the Wildwoman Archetype, it brings a phase of "crisis in action" and marks a time for breaking free of past restrictions. It is a phase of radical, instinctive movement, made for the sake of survival, evolution, freedom. It wakens our primal hunger— the cry of Life, itself.

SPRING EQUINOX:
(March 21)

This seasonal holy day proclaims the re-birth of Earth— its release from the dark days of winter death into spring's budding creation, when life breaks out. Rain refreshes soils that open to the increasing light and warmth. Spring festivals mark a time of rejoicing in a world renewed. Eggs and rabbits symbolize the season's fertility and sacred mysteries.

GIBBOUS MOON
BELTANE

Gibbous Moon is the "brimming cup" phase. It rises close to sunset, its face radiant, nearing culmination. This marks a time of rising hopes, increasing confidence. Enthusiasm, excitement, creative imagination are heightened, as the anticipation of reward rouses determination to succeed. Focus turns toward finding meaning and purpose in life, seeking constructive answers to problems, throwing light on questions posed about ourselves and our world.

BELTANE:
(April 30, May 1)
May Eve. Summer's Edge. By May Day, the storms of spring have subsided, and Nature unfolds, releasing her newborns in calmness and confidence. Festivities honor growth, outreach, merriment. Trees are symbolic of this holy period world-wide— exhibited in the May Pole, around which we dance to twine our dreams.

FULL MOON
SUMMER SOLSTICE

At the full of moon, the sun and moon hover directly across from each other, balanced on opposite sides of the earth. As Earth floats between them, bathed in their magnetic glow, she responds with all her senses. All creatures are seduced by the charismatic face of the Full Moon, for to be "moonstruck" means you are goddess-blessed with love's magic. This is the Lover's moon, awakening all creatures and people to relate to that which lies outside of themselves. It marks a phase in which we reach forth to connect, to touch, and to embrace the Other.

SUMMER SOLSTICE:
(June 21)
Midsummer.
The longest day. Earth blossoms, her creatures court, and Life sings a song of attraction, desire and beauty. The height of solar power has been honored with shrines, temples, and standing stone circles since prehistoric times: all built to register the moment when sunlight penetrates the womb of Earth, conceiving renewed life.

DISSEMINATING MOON
LAMMAS

Rising shortly after the sun has gone down, the disseminating moon remains strong in light, but slightly misshapen— gradually veiling her face, deflecting her light. Just so, the Companion Archetype deflates her own importance in order to lend a portion of her power to something outside of herself. This is a phase in which we share our gifts, disseminate our knowledge, and pass the wealth around. It is a time for generating inter-relationships; for telling our stories to help each other grow and co-create a viable, sustainable, productive life.

LAMMAS:
(August 2)
Summer's end. This is the season of fruitfulness and fertility. It is the time for festivals of First Fruits Harvest— a time of abundance and prosperity. Now we open our hearts to share with others and to give thanks for the riches and blessings provided us by the earth in return for our labor.

9

SECOND HALF-MOON
AUTUMN EQUINOX

Rising in the depth of night, the waning half-moon floats high above in the early light of dawn. Resembling the blade of a battle ax, or the hoof-print of a warrior's steed, it marks the phase when a mission must be completed. It is the point in any cycle where we achieve our aims or we must let them go. Consequently, it is a time of revolt against limiting beliefs; a rebellion against out-dated ideas. The Warrior within helps us discover what we search for, overcome what obstructs our progress, defeat what threatens our liberty. The Warrior's moon stands guard, reminding us to prepare ourselves for our own daily skirmishes with life.

**AUTUMN EQUINOX:
(September 21)**
Mid-fall. Equal day and night. Dark begins to increase, and light wanes. It is the time to reap the final harvest, to gather in what has been grown, to stockpile provisions for fallow months to come, and to fortify defenses against winter's blasts.

BALSAMIC MOON
SAMHAIN

Rising in the wee hours of morning, the darkest hours before dawn, a boat-shaped waning crescent moon drifts on the horizon, arriving to carry us to a land of mystery. It is the time when we dream our deepest dreams. Unseen, the moon leads the sun through the day's transit across the heavens— like the mystical Wise Women of enchanted lands led heroes to their destiny across the deep waters of Time. Named for a plant known for its soothing balm, the moon's Balsamic phase is a time for healing wounds. We are reminded that death is merely the doorway into the next life, and we may rejoice in a momentary reprieve from earthly struggles.

SAMHAIN:
(October 31)
Halloween. Winter's eve. The cold winds wail and sigh among bared branches. The veil between worlds grows thin, so we see how death and decline are but the shadow-sides of birth and growth— necessary for life's cycles to continue unbroken. Festivals of the Dead honor ancestors and call forth strange wonders.

The Goddess Wheel

BALSAMIC MOON WISE WOMAN

Healing
Sacrifice
Mystery

NEW MOON MOTHER

Containment
Rebirth
Renewal

Innocence
Curiosity
Playfulness

SECOND HALF MOON WARRIOR

Courage
Passion
Dedication

DISSEMINATING MOON COMPANION

Equality
Cooperation
Mutuality

FIRST HALF MOON WILDWOMAN

Action
Survival
Freedom

FULL MOON LOVER

Attraction
Desire
Fulfillment

GIBBOUS MOON MUSE

Creativity
Expression
Mastery

Grandmother Moon has 8 Faces and 24 Masks

I call the moon "grandmother" because she is the original symbol of feminine mysteries known throughout Earth. The moon goes through a continually repeating, never failing, ever-changing cycle of shapes, sizes, degrees of light or darkness. As we watch her progress through the heavens each month, she mirrors our own changing moods with her enigmatic presence. She abides at the core of most feminine spiritual traditions and teachings.

The archetypes I name are envisioned in phases of the moon, sequenced to correlate symbolically with Woman's natural attunement to the monthly progression, and emphasizing the central significance of cycles in women's lives. However, although I present these images in a lunar sequence, they don't necessarily constellate in our earthly lives in such an orderly parade.

Grandmother Moon has eight faces— eight defined 3.5-day phases in her monthly cycle of 28 days. Within the eight-phase lunar cycle, a 3-beat rhythm — waxing/whole/waning— has become central to moon-lore. These three stages symbolize a sacred trinity, reflecting the perpetual turning of the wheel of life: past, present, future— growth, ripening, decay— opening, filling, emptying. In this book, the threefold rhythm is repeated by three "masks" or "character roles" worn by each of the eight Archetypes as they initiate, sustain, and release their particular female sexual-spiritual Essence.

First, her waxing mask represents an emerging and growthful period of life. It may be seen as the "simplest" expression of the type, most easily recognized, and generally accepted by society. Second, her whole mask represents the culmination and fulfillment periods of life, experienced as a fecund, carnal period when she is most evident in her purpose and power— the boldest expression of the type, and often challenged or controlled by society. Third, her waning mask represents life's periods of dispersion and withdrawal, experienced as a release, regeneration, and re-visioning. This deeply inward energy is penetrating, shadowy, and mysterious— a dormant force— and therefore, feared, denigrated, and shunned by society.

We can all recognize parts of ourselves in these images.

Nurture / Rebirth / Renew

The Mother Archetype bears all others in her vast, prodigious lineage. Her body is the receptacle, the container for all vital energies in their emerging, growing forms. The Mother Archetype begins the cycle of our creative spiritual evolution, but she also reveals the mystery of our return and renewal through death.

At New Moon I am the Mother with her Child. My children are of all species and forms, as I bring them forth through my Creation. Do you remember when you were full with a new dream, laboring to bring it to life? A child, a song, a business, a book... I was there with you then.

I teach you to observe the cycles and rhythms of your body, as they harmonize with those of Earth— which is my body. I am the Divine Mother, pregnant with the Holy things of life, conceived in every woman's womb. I am the Grandmother, bringing the wisdom of age, helping you accept changes when your moon-blood ceases, and your powers of nurture deepen to embrace life's moment.

At my moon-phase, the sun enfolds the moon in radiant daylight veils, while the night is pierced by stars in fecund darkness— where all New Life begins.

Mother Earth = Containment

Divine Mother = Nourishment

Grandmother = Reassurance

Mother Archetype

Spiraling
A swirling
Goddess circle
by Kanii Weiss,
10/96

15

Earth remains ever the prototypical Female, recreated in the fertility cycles and bodies of all women. The bond we inherit through our physical bodies to the earth connects us to all her creatures forever. Deep in our bones, we remember our sacred earthy origins.

Mother Earth represents the bounteous fertility and propagation of the planet we live on. In this painting, she is Gaia, goddess ever-birthing, ever giving and receiving life for the creatures living on, and in, her body. She is the bearer of the world on which we live, and is, herself, within all of her creation. Her smile bestows warmth and sunshine, her tears bring refreshing rain, her eyes reflect the sparkling night skies. At her roots gather the creatures of plenty and persistence and prosperity: the rabbit and the turtle— legendary tortoise and hare— guarding eggs that will hatch yet more abundance.

The stories about Mother Earth are found throughout all her continents and on all the ocean's islands. The earth's waters are the source of all life herein. The oceans depths, the rivers lengths, and the glacial melted lakes perpetually spew forth Mother Earth's amniotic fluids, bearing ever-renewed life. Yet, she lives in great peril from the lowest of her creatures— humankind— the last to be created, and the least respectful of her great good bounty. Mother Earth needs our nurture now.

Invocation to Mother Earth:

Help me be grounded in your strength and enduring sensibility.
Let my body mirror the abundance of your generous gifts.
Let my roots reach into the depths of your nurturing, all-knowing spirit.

I pray to preserve and protect the earth.

SUN IN TAURUS: Security, Grounding, Roots.
TAROT, XXI = "WORLD" Completion, Centrality, Source.

MOTHER EARTH

The Divine Mother, with her child, stands for the ultimate bond between two souls: a merging of carnal with sacred energy to create new life through the mystical experiences of birthing and nourishing a relationship. A Divine Mother's love reaches far beyond the personal, to the profound, the all-embracing; beyond plain reality to inscrutable mystery. The nurturance of divine motherhood manifests as tough-love.

She represents the Virgin mother— the Madonna, Mary, of Christian legend, the great Egyptian goddess, Isis, and their counterparts of other arcane myth. In this painting, she sits by the water, offering her nurturing bounty to the holy child in her arms. A Guardian-Angel Mother and her Angel Child stand beside her— representatives of all generations in the never-ending lineage of our first ancestress. In the trees and on the water, representatives of mothers in Nature keep vigil at this serene nativity. The Divine Mother's halo radiates the rainbow— a bridge between heaven and earth.

The Divine Mother is virgin, for she belongs to no man, but has conceived her child in sacred ritual ceremony— whereby the babe symbolizes the union of love and peace ever-renewed through the womb of the goddess. She may be the legendary Mary Magdalen, who is said to have been consort to the avatar, Jesus, and bore his child secretly, after escaping to France for sanctuary. This child— a girl— is destined to carry forth the goddess lineage in the very shadow of patriarchy.

Invocation to Divine Mother:

Help me demonstrate care-giving nurture to all of life.
Let my relationships with children— and with the child in myself—
grow in gentle appreciation for the wisdom of innocence.
Help me curb my own appetites,
so that I may more generously nourish others.

I pray for fertile conception, robust pregnancy, facile birth,
and healthy progeny.

SUN IN CANCER: Receptivity, Nourishment, Containment, Guardedness
TAROT, III - "EMPRESS" Humane love, Providence, Nourishing relationship

DIVINE MOTHER

Grandmother guides our passage as she spins the yarns that give meaning to the confusing changes in our lives. Like a fairy godmother, she helps us look at life with a fresh eye— through her clarified vision of hind-sight. She knows the secret to survival is to let go, let be, and move on.

In this painting, the Guardian Grandmother with angel wings serenades her creatures at the event of a holy and heavenly nativity. The animals have come to pay homage, as the infant goddess pays respect to them, in turn. The baby goddess inherits her beauty and wisdom from her holy feminine lineage, and Grandmother goddess imparts the stories that will guide her in her life's pursuits.

Perhaps, this angelic and youthful Grandmother is especially meant to reveal how our ageless wisdom follows no set stereotype, fits no preconceived notions of "proper" appearance, style, background, or chronological age. We can each call forth Grandmother goddess, from within ourselves, at any stage of our life. Her good-humored wisdom always comforts, always assures, and always leads us home.

Grandmother is the Good Witch and the Fairy Godmother of all our childhood fantasy tales. She is the beatific one who bestows life-preserving magic to her progeny. It is her profound purpose to remind us that beauty never dies, but is re-cycled ever renewed, age upon age. Therefore, every death is the beginning of a new life.

Invocation to the Grandmother:

Help me to accept my aging body and the fact of death as an integral part of life. Help me to believe that my experiences in life give me knowledge of worth to pass on to others.

I pray to accept major life-passages gracefully.

SUN IN VIRGO: Practical experience, Problem-solving, Teaching, Healing
TAROT: XIII = "DEATH" Transformation, Conscious Rebirth.

GRANDMOTHER

Play / Learn / Practice

The Maiden is core to all others, for she embodies the soul's dream.
In her world, the magic of make-believe prevails.
The freedom to explore our fantasies as children,
gives us self-confidence to pursue our dreams as women.

At Crescent Moon I am the Maiden, pure and innocent, gathering sensations and fantasies in a paradise of worldly delights. I am the Good daughter, inner soul of the Mother, learning the art of merging. I am the Naughty daughter, seducing my parents, learning the skill of separating. I am the Orphan teenage daughter, favorite of the gods, stumbling blindly into the mysteries of puberty and adolescence.

Eagerly seeking playmates, while hiding from villainous beasts, I am vulnerable and foolish, sensitive and curious— a contradictory mix of potentials, as yet unfulfilled. I rule the worlds of make-believe and fantasy, and I teach you how to play. Do you remember when you giggled in delight at the simple joy of being alive? I was there with you then, and also when you screeched in terror at imagined frights.

My waxing crescent moon emerges in mysterious beauty, glimpsed briefly, following sunset— and often accompanied by Venus, glimmering nearby as the Evening Star— the Wishing Star. You may make a wish and dare to dream what your heart most desires, for I will help you believe that whatever you wish for could come true.

Good Girl = Innocence
Naughty Girl = Curiosity
Orphan Maiden = Cleverness

Maiden Archetype

The Good Girl represents ever-renewed virginity, ever-present maidenhood, hidden within every woman. She is the part of us that wishes to please, to keep harmony in order to have fun and feel happy. Her energy is light-hearted, optimistic— and she fervently believes in Magic.

In the painting, the little girl blithely swings, as her puppy sleeps peacefully beneath the tree, guarding her hat and shoes. But her cat, in the basket, senses the dangerous elements encroaching on their paradisiacal playground, which lies perilously close to the dark forest-edge. There stands the wily fox, amused by this vulnerable trio, and debating how best to mount a surprise chase. The snake, however, may be a protector-goddess in disguise, ready to foil the fox's plans.

Perhaps, this innocent swinging maiden is a modern-day Kore, idling away her springtime youth, oblivious to the inevitable abduction to come. She is tripled in the painting, appearing as three times herself. The stories of innocent maidens foreshadow a division from childhood into adolescence, and then into womanhood. But, the young maiden perceives a magical world, where all wishes are heard by the fairies in the tree, and can come true. Even the frights of the forest, with tricky wolves or foxes, are part of the drama of her make-believe adventure. They, as yet, present no real threat to her trusting innocence, which is her form of power.

Invocation to Good Girl:
Help me to find joy in the simple pleasures of my daily life.
Let me bring happiness to others by the warmth of my smile,
and through my genuine delight in the world. Help me to
engage the innocent child within, to attain basic trust and
acceptance of myself.

I pray to increase and sustain vitality, youthfulness, and self-esteem.

SUN IN LIBRA: Diplomacy, Grace, Charm, Celebrative interactions
TAROT: XIX = "SUN" Happiness, Warmth, Playful attitude

GOOD GIRL

The pre-adolescent Maiden feeds her curiosity from an unlimited, unquestioned sense of her own autonomy. She plays all the roles in her make-believe dramas, exploring her own androgynous potentials. She dares to disobey, in order to test limits and discover boundaries of her world. The Naughty Girl Maiden helps us laugh at our mistakes, tease away our fears, face life with a grin, take whatever comes our way and make the best of it.

The pre-pubescent Maiden Naughty Girl is not bad, in the pejorative sense, but possesses the daring-combined-with-innocence required to pursue all paths, open all doors, and investigate all containers she comes upon. This is the "tomboy" androgynous maiden, who is free to experiment with all sides of her nature. In the painting, she is in the midst of a tempest, which she has accidentally raised by opening the secret box and releasing its power. Storm winds stir the waves, tossing the sailboat on the water, while lightning flashes and thunder booms. Yet, the setting sun peeks from behind the clouds and the rising crescent moon is accompanied by the maiden's wishing star.

Here, we may have Pandora in pigtails and jeans. Her curiosity prompts her to open the forbidden container. But it is merely a shoebox of childhood seaside treasures. No evil lurks here, but only the wonder of Nature's gifts. The storm is invigorating and titillating— energizing the Maiden's magical world.

Invocation to Naughty Girl:
Help me to let go of unnecessary controls over my spirit.
Help me to sing and dance to the music of life all around me.
Help me to join in on the games offered by my daily encounters
with all my fellow creatures on earth.

I pray to banish guilt and express myself honestly.

MOON IN GEMINI: Versatility, Curiosity, Amusing Communications
TAROT: XII = "HANGED ONE" Surrender of ego to heart's power

NAUGHTY GIRL

The adolescent young woman throws off protective wrappings of girlhood, to expose herself to life's dangerous adventures, and thereby, discover her true identity. The Orphan Maiden's adroit flair for drama provides her with inventiveness to play the roles demanded for a skillful passage through adolescence.

In this painting, she sits at the water's edge, embracing a unicorn, who gazes dreamily at its own reflection. Here, the Orphan Maiden appears unreal, fairy-like, merely a mirage of her former autonomous girl-self, with but a hint of her future woman-power. She is beautiful, but insubstantial— fragile in her blossoming erotic passion. Yet, therein lies the secret to her special power, for she can take on the character and form of whatever helps her survive a malevolent culture's attacks against her innocent beauty.

Beyond the mists that veil her magical world of illusion, we see a man on horseback, riding from the castle in the hills— a symbol of the patriarchal world. Is this her abductor, coming to snatch her from her sheltered sanctuary? Or, perhaps, it is a messenger of the goddess, coming to warn her of other dangers. Or is he the knight who will rescue her from the clutches of an evil sorceress? This Maiden may be Daphne, or Io, or any of many nymphs and maidens, chased by rapacious gods, tricked by villainous brutes, but ultimately transformed by the fates to attain immortality as selected daughters of the goddess.

Invocation to Orphan Maiden:
Help me keep my loving spirit safe within the harbor of
my heart, while I venture into the world of unknown dangerous
opportunities to discover my true self and purpose.

I pray to find blessed initiation into the female
blood mysteries and honor my woman- power.

MOON IN ARIES; Risk-taker, Assertive search for belonging, Initiate
TAROT: XX = "JUDGEMENT" Open-hearted consciousness

ORPHAN MAIDEN

Survive / Revel / Exploit

At First Quarter Moon, I am the untamable Wild-woman, free and uninhibited, with sometimes bloody tooth and claw. I passionately follow the instincts of Nature to give elemental expression to the primal urges of erotic life. Do you remember when you have let your hair down and dared to shout, scream, or laugh very loudly, without concern for what others might think? I was your source of ecstasy and power.

I am Dame Nature, the Madwoman, and the Whore— all despised by the world, feared for their ruthless, uncivilized, lusty energy. Dancing to a frenzy, I have led many a daemonic orgy in ancient ages past— and I would enjoy coming forth in the company of women today. But I am recognized and respected only by the street-wise, and by the so-called "crazy ones" who commune and prowl with the animals.

My moon-phase is a time to take action— to break out of constraints and declare your Spirit free. Like the animals, in whom I dwell most easily, I live only in the moment, with no regret for past, nor hope for future. My passion is here. Now. I roar. I screech. I howl. I dance in ecstatic celebration of erotic Life.

The Wild-woman is the animal part of us who roars, howls, snarls, screeches, with untamed primitive passion. She is the keeper of an inner bestiary, the choreographer of a psychic circus of barely contained passions, waiting to be un-caged. In her profound madness, the Wild-woman shakes our complacency, awakens our enthusiasm to enter the tragic and comic struggles of life.

Dame Nature = Ruthlessness

Maenad = Bawdiness

Whore = Opportunism

Wild Woman Archetype

Wild-woman Dame Nature won't succumb to the rules of mankind. She answers to the voice of the Elements alone, for none other speaks her tongue. Throughout the earth, the voice of Dame Nature calls, and our deep inner Wild Self hears.

Dame Nature presides over all that cannot be tamed. In this painting, she sits, horned and masked, amid her companion Elementals, who dance, prance, frolic, and cavort around her. Winged fairies flit about, gentle as whispers. Mischievous naiads surf the waterfall and lounge upon tree branches. Serious, ageless gnomes accompany the Dame's pipe-dream, while guileless pixies scamper through the magic holly-vines at her feet. In the distance, the Firebird soars beyond the fiery volcano of its birth, and a magic dragon sea-serpent sails the diamond-bright waters below.

We spy upon a tranquil moment in an often tumultuous world, where trespassers can cause bedlam. Beware the gaze of Dame Nature, for she is capricious, and can turn her wrath raging upon us in an instant. Yet, she produces exhilarating vicissitudes that can open all our senses to the ephemeral sights, scents and sounds of life-evolving. Perhaps, this is a representative of Irish Fairy Queen, Maeve. Or she may be the great Hawaiian volcano goddess, Pele, awaiting the return of her lost lover. Dame Nature's flute, akin to the magical Pipes of Pan, calls lost lovers through the storm, bringing them to each other's arms, or to death

Invocation to Dame Nature:
Help me learn to hear your voice and appreciate your
elemental magic. Help me open up to the storms of life, with
a willingness to be tossed in your winds of cleansing power.
Let me brave the unknown forces, in order to heal the
wounds of a sexist culture.

I pray to effect purification, after a period of struggle and difficulty.

MOON IN AQUARIUS: Eccentric, Visionary, Non-conformist, Unpredictable
TAROT: XXI = "WORLD" Cosmic Energies, Dance with Nature

Dame Nature's Elementals
2-7-99 - Karin Weiss

DAME NATURE

The Maenad-Madwoman has an instinctual erotic power that amplifies our voice, escalates our pace, animates all our creative expression. But, it is she whom we try hardest to suppress, deny, eradicate— for she is our Crazy Self. The madwoman within compels our attention through acts beyond our wildest dreams, in thoughts we would never harbor waking, but obsessively cherish in sleep.

In this painting, shameless, outrageous, alluring women dance, sing, and play in the wild with animal companions. The crescent moon glows orange through a fiery sunset, reflecting on the burnished skin and ruddy hair of these fairy maidens in their green glade. Irish are they? I would guess they are daughters of the great Banshee, herself. Oblivious to the moral judgments of civil society, these daughters of the Wild-woman hark only to their physical senses and spirited instincts. They represent the truly free aspect of women's erotic spirit— that which dares ride the winds of fate in the wake of a ravenous and chaotic dream-lover.

These are women with the powers that men dread: the power of female orgasm, orgy, and insatiable sexual appetite. As followers of Dionysos, Bachus, and Pan— gods of sexual revelry and intoxication— the Maenads can be clowns of the universe, capering foolishly to the brink of disaster. Yet, they come to no harm, for they are merely paying respect to the god of revelry— giving themselves over to the secrets of joy-possessed.

Invocation to Maenad-Madwoman:
Help me release the untamed creature within me to dance in the night without fear. Let me open myself to my own crazy mystery, and embrace my own madness that must be loosed to heal.

I pray to banish feelings of timidity and separate myself from traps of propriety.

MOON IN PISCES: Intuitive, Psychic, Led by Dreams, Comfort in the Fantastic
TAROT: XVIII = "MOON" Ocean Tides and Menstrual Cycles

MAENAD/MADWOMAN

The Whore stands for Sex, stark and naked. Her sexuality is her power in a world that is ruled by hypocritical, rapacious, profligate men— and she meets them at their crudest level. To her, sex is nothing romantic, it is just a job. Her services are in constant demand, even while damned and defiled.. Her history is seminal to all women's sexual emancipation, for it reaches back to our beginnings. The "oldest profession" originates in the earliest religious rites, where harlots and hierodules of the ancient world were an essential civilizing force. By the prostitute's cultured skills of eroticism, mankind was humanized.

In this painting, standing naked in a blooming bower, the Whore shares the shimmering fruit of sensual enlightenment with her venerable consort and companion, the serpent— phallic, fecund creature of original mystery and primal cunning. Together, promiscuous and sexually knowledgeable, the whore and her sinuous cohort strike terror in the hearts of so-called "decent" people— those with senses too timid to meet openly the wanton gaze of undiluted sex.

This is Jahi the Whore, unknown to westerners. Her tale is told in Persian Zoroastrian scriptures, where she is said to have seduced the first man in her primal garden, and thus introduced sex into the world. She was a revered goddess in the permissive joyful worship of women, but reviled under ensuing inhibited patriarchal asceticism. Of course, we do know Jahi by another name— Eve.

Invocation to the Whore:
Help me recognize my own habits of exploitive opportunism.
Let me use my erotic wisdom to achieve important goals,
but not to become a victim to my sexuality,
nor a slave to another's.

I pray to banish sexual shame and
withstand negative judgments of others.

MOON IN SCORPIO: Penetrating, Transforming, Seductive, Intense, Vengeful
TAROT: IV = "EMPEROR" Patriarchy's Dangers, Sex for Power

Jahi In The Garden
Karin Weiss 6/21/99

WHORE

Laughter / Performance / Inspiration

At Gibbous moon, I am the Dreaming Muse, waking your imagination with evocative songs, enchanting visions, and enthralling ideas. I inspire you to create. To enrich. To amuse. To give meaning to your daily life. My energy surges like a siren's song through your veins, enticing you into the rapture of your own creativity.

I am the Clown, inciting enthusiasm for the games of life; helping you to communicate what you believe, see, think, feel. I am the Star, helping you master skills and talents; an entertainer, who dramatizes your hopes and fears. I am the Siren, who captures Soul, through art, poetry, song, and dance— evoking the unspeakable, the dreaded, the hoped-for dream. Remember when you created something from your heart? When you competed with skill and excellence at a talent you love? I inspired you then, showing that creative and erotic energy are One.

My lunar phase expands and fills out the form of whatever has been growing within your imagination. I help you claim your unique power of self-expression, self-esteem, self-confidence. I inspire your self-determination to succeed.

The Muse rules the power of evocation— she is the calling-spirit. Poetry wells up from the roots of our soul, imbued with her passion. On wings of inspiration, she sails above our limited ego-minds, to show us the splendor inherent in all Creation. The inner Muse drums the rhythms of a universal cadence that leads us into an ecstatic dance with Life.

Clown = Good Humor

Star = Self-Mastery

Siren = Imagination

Muse Archetype

The Clown is witness to the capacity for soulful play. She teaches that, in the great web woven from time's memories lies the power to heal all wounds with laughter, wit, and good humor. She helps us recapture our appreciation for the ridiculous, to reclaim our own sublime comic-self who looks at life and chuckles. She reminds us that laughter is always good medicine, for it keeps us young at heart.

The Clown-Muse rides "bareback" with all puns intended. She brings laughter and good humor into our daily lives by means of her tricks and jokes. In this painting, she is a "spider grandmother" sitting in the web of life, catching the grinning moon in one hand, while a chattering magpie sits on her shoulder and gossips in her ear. She laughs at the absurdity of civil rules of conduct and sits spread-legged, flashing a clown's comic face, composed of her nipples, belly-button, and vulva. A butterfly in her hand promises transformation, and a spiraled shell on her breast holds secrets of female power. The bear gazes with serene amusement at the those who look in on them.

Here is the goddess of laughter and lifted skirts, Baubo, who brought mother Demeter out of mourning for the loss of Kore, her daughter, to womanhood. In just this way, old women of wisdom— within and outside of ourselves— can help us to find the humor in everyday trials and tribulations; bring out our laughter at times of boredom or despair.

Invocation to the Clown:

Help me open myself to the jokes and comedies of life
all around me every day. Let me learn to see the humor,
even in tragedy, and to make of life a continual source of
amusement and delight. Help me avoid stupidity, while
enjoying the absurdities of my own foolish being.

I pray to mend broken relationships with good humor.

SUN IN GEMINI: Versatility, Humor, Communicative skill, Gossip
TAROT: 0 = "FOOL" Infinite Possibilities, Divine Laughter

CLOWN

With the guidance of our inner Star, we have the power to rise above limitations and reach for the stars. The Muse Star carries the torch that lights our creative fire. She elevates our level of aspiration and magnifies our performance. She calls us to stretch our limits, master our craft, triumph in our field, and win the rewards of excellence.

In this painting, rising in flames of glory, the Star seems unbelievable, unreachable, and unimpeachable. She rides the fiery dragon of feminine powers unleashed, which is assumed by patriarchal forces to be evil, but is essentially healing. The starry heavens pale in the glow of this goddess-light. The dove of peace wings its way, sheltered in the cool breeze of the Star's self-confidence. She wears a rainbow-snake, like a ribbon of shimmering satin, a symbol of all-transforming, ever-regenerating, and perfected power.

This may be the goddess of wisdom, Sophia, who is God's own muse. She rides the skies in veils of arcane knowledge, and disperses creative talents to those with wit and stamina to fly with her into the un-inhaled ethers, the untried heights of imagination. She may be one of the starry goddesses— Astarte, Ishtar, Atargatis, Esther, or Tara— all icons of inspired creativity and dedicated devotion to high ideals. The Star within every woman contributes light to the star-fire egg cradled in this cool-hot goddess' outstretched hand. In her other hand, she has the dragon— guardian of the "Flaming Pearl" (spiritual perfection)— by its tail.

Invocation to the Star:

Help me perfect my talents and bring them forth to enrich
my life and that of others. Let me believe in my ability to
achieve my best, and to perform without false modesty
or debilitating self-doubt. Help me to overcome my fear
of genuine fulfillment.

I pray to perform my very best, and
experience confidence without arrogance.

SUN IN LEO: Dramatic, Confident, Flamboyant, Magnanimous, Arrogant
TAROT: XIV = "TEMPERENCE" Balanced, Centered Integrity

Wise
Woman
Ascending   Karin Weiss
                10/12/92

THE STAR

The Siren Muse is a sorceress. Her song is mesmerizing, captivating, enchanting. She beckons, and we jump the ship of status-quo, diving to the depths of an inner psychic sea that reveals treasures visible, uniquely, to our own soul. The Siren distracts us from the assigned order of things, and calls us to pursue secret inner longings, faraway visions, untried solutions, unexplored horizons. We hear her voice above the din of our daily life, enticing us from routine tasks, to follow an instinctual trail into our personal Dream.

The Muse, as Siren, can take myriad forms, including those of fairies and angels. In this painting she appears as a mermaid, rising through swirling blue waters of a magical island cove. Like all creatures of the ocean's depths, the mermaid is associated with dangerous otherworldly powers that are used to trap and enchant innocent men. Perhaps she is the sea-nymph, Calypso, swimming toward the Greek hero, Odysseus, drifting becalmed in her mystical waters. Captivated on her island, he will forget how to make war, and learn how to make love.

Like fabled naiads in wishing wells, Aladdin's magical djinni, or the holy grail quested by knights of old – the Siren Muse presents a "calling" for heroes to find and unite with their own female principle in order to become whole. Perhaps this is Minne, a Celtic mermaid muse-goddess (her name means *love's desire*) evoked by troubadours in ballads for Medieval court-ladies, where seduction was the name of the game.

Invocation to the Siren:

Help me to accept that I, too, have the ability to enchant and
entice others to my desires, and help me remember that my
wishes are not always best for others. Yet help me dare to
follow the call of my own dreams, in order to discover the
deeper purposes and meanings of my life.

I pray that I can use my charms to attract
others to my just and fair cause.

MOON IN SAGITTARIUS: Expansive life-view, Exaggerated ideals, Indulgent
TAROT: X = "WHEEL OF FORTUNE" Cyclic call. Turning tides, Destiny's spin

The Siren Calls
Karen Weiss — 1-3-99

THE SIREN

Attraction / Desire / Captivation

At Full Moon I am the Lover within you. I am the source of your romantic desire, your hunger for intimate contact with another. Through your body, I bring you the thrill of Eros. Do you remember your first crush? Your first date? Your first kiss? I was there with you each time, kindling the flame of desire and heightening your passion.

I am the Beauty Queen, admired and adored from afar. I am the Charming Sweetheart, held near and dear and pure. And I am the Vamp Temptress, tantalizing, wickedly wanton. I am revered and feared as the epitome of sexual magnetism. My loins throb with the pulse of ardent rapture. My eyes shed the tears of lost loves.

My glorious moon-phase illuminates the night for all lovers, and brings sexual power to its full evocative magic. It marks a moment when energies are aroused in howling wolves and "lunatics" of all species, and when the Fairy Folk come out to enchant mortals. Thus, men grow wary and fearful at my intense mystery. Yet, none can resist my charms.

The Lover is the part of us for whom the poems are composed and the songs are sung. She is the mystique of beauty and the object of desire. She holds our heart in her hands and thrums its beat at the center of our soul. She wields powers of attraction, affection, and attachment that can sear our soul. Even so, she strengthens our hearts through an alchemy of suffering, and we learn that romantic love thrives on tragedy.

Beauty Queen = Charisma

Sweetheart = Enchantment

Vamp = Temptation

The lover Archetype

The Beauty Queen stands magnificent and proud within every woman's soul, commanding attention, demanding respect, eliciting admiration. She is that part in us that knows we are beautiful, regardless how society may judge our looks or others fail to take us in with their gaze. As the subject of endless poems, songs, artwork, and dreams, beauty remains ever elusive, always subjective, ever contained only in the eye or mind of its beholder. Yet, for those with all senses attuned, nothing can be absolutely ugly, for something beautiful resides within the heart of all things.

Three great narcissistic Beauties once vied for the prize of a golden apple, awarded by one conceited prince, named Paris. In this painting we observe them in a modern parody of the Original Beauty Pageant. Goddesses, Aphrodite, Hera, and Athena, each attends, dressed in finery characteristic of her nature. In this elegant promenade, each goddess is accompanied by her representative bird: Aphrodite's love-doves nest in her luxurious tresses. Hera's peacock preens, draped across her stately shoulder. And Athena's wise little owl watches serenely, perched upon her sturdy hand. The owl still stands for Athena's artifice, the peacock for Hera's pride, and the doves for Aphrodite's sexual desire. Paris awarded the apple to Aphrodite. Some men still choose sexual conquest over political or martial fame. But, beauty, like sexual attraction, is ever dangerous, ever capricious, and rarely lasting as first judged.

Invocation to the Beauty Queen:
Help me believe in my own beauty and wear it with grace.
Let me learn that how attractive I appear is a measure of
how good I let myself feel. Help me avoid vanity,
but grow in self-appreciation.

I pray to be essentially beautiful, without pretensions.

MOON IN LIBRA: Charm and diplomacy; Comfort in beauty; Vanity
TAROT: XVII = "STAR" Grace brings love; Hope and trust in self-healing

Original Beauty Contest
Karin E. Weiss, 1-18-99

BEAUTY QUEEN

Clinging to illusions of promised happiness, gazing after phantoms of a wistful paradise, the Sweetheart beckons us to follow her blindly into affairs of the heart. Romance catches us in a timeless moment. Falling into Eros' thrall, we willingly forego all past memories and future possibilities for the pleasure of love's fleeting instant. For a space of time we regress— we delight in the power of wishes, dreams, and miracles. We fall in love with the illusions of Love.

Here are the ephemeral Sweethearts of mythology— Psyche and Eros— in the eternal embrace of enchanted captivation. In the painting, he appears in the form of a divine butterfly, accompanied by an entourage of Psyche's own spirit-manifestations. But might his antennae, pointed ears, and non-human coloring suggest that this divinity, while handsome, is in some way beastly, critterly— dare we say it?— buggy? (Certainly lovers can appear rather so.) But, their fanciful, playful mood belies a tragic fate. These lovers, floating so buoyantly above the weight of the world, flitting carelessly among dream spirits, seem oblivious to future downfalls.

Once upon a time, when this tale was born, lovers lived forever by dying in each other's arms. Therein lies the source of comic tragedy in romantic love, for lovers long to go together into the heavenly ethers, never to come back down to earth and face humble, mundane realities.

Invocation to the Sweetheart:
Help me to find the romance I desire in my life.
Let me see it when it arrives, and not be blinded
by foolish, unrealistic notions of "perfect" love.
Help me open my heart to the pains, as
well as the pleasures, of romance.

I pray to love well and fully.

MOON IN LEO: Drama about love and romance; Open-hearted; Narcissistic
TAROT: 0 = "FOOL" Blissfully unconscious; Blind trust in ideals; Childish faith

Psyche + Eros Butterflies
Karen E. Weiss — 1/18/99

THE SWEETHEART

The Vamp is a darkly savvy sexual woman. The Lover, as Vamp, is a brash, cold aspect of female sexual magnetism. Her more genteel title is the *Femme Fatale*— the deadly woman who sometimes leads men to their ruin.

In the painting, Beauty dances with the Beast. He is the Horned God of Celtic myth, who will first be worshipped for his fertile manhood, and then slain to preserve and anoint his progeny. She dances with him, both to honor his crowning and to betray his demise. But the Horned God is a willing victim, voluntarily entering the Vamp's venomous chamber to lie in her fierce embrace, knowing that in doing so he writes his own death warrant. It is an ancient and complex ritual we find difficult to comprehend, yet we re-enact it regularly without knowing.

The Vamp dares dance (and sleep) with the dangerous man, the villain, the potential killer. She does so partly for the thrill of taming his brute nature. But she does so ultimately to gain advantage over him, to deflect his offensive ambitions. By seducing him, she disarms his weapon, renders him vulnerable in his own lair, caught in his own trap. This modern dancing vixen is ancestress to many a famous Vamp in myth and history: Delilah, Salome, Judith, Esther, and Tamar from biblical tales; Cleopatra, Brynhilde, Mata Hari, and the Cat Woman, from secular legends. Always, we find the Vamp's stories reveal her heroic courage, although her name becomes defiled by history.

Invocation to the Vamp:
Help me dare to use my charms for the good
of my higher purpose. Let me understand that
seduction is a double-edged instrument for good or evil;
that I can employ it for, or against, my best interests.
Help me overcome my fear of my own seductive power.

I pray for courage to face up to betrayed and broken love.

MOON IN TAURUS: Sensual physical pleasure; Security in tough persistence
TAROT: XV = "DEVIL" Attraction for personal gain; Ego-driven cravings

Dancing with the
Horned God — Xavier E Weiss, 1/24/99

THE VAMP

Trust / Share / Support

At Disseminating moon I am the loyal Companion, who thrives on the power of partnership— Matron, Matriarch, bosom of mature womanly love. I am the Handmaiden who forgoes personal desires for the duties of loving service. I am the Mate / Wife, claiming title and commitment within, or without, marriage. I am the Sister / Friend, sharing interests, causes, goals in a communal world.

I counsel fairness and cooperation to create harmony in relationships. I celebrate the fruitful prospects of fertile partnerships. Do you recognize the power of working cooperatively, side by side, with others whom you respect and love as equals? I am the source of that power in you. Do you remember dreaming of marriage, as a girl or woman? I hold forth that ideal to those who choose it— yet, I remind you that marriage is a serious undertaking that goes far beyond the naively romantic wedding-dream. I admonish those who would make of marriage an "ownership" contract, that we have no rights of possession over another person's being.

My moon-phase represents shared blessings, and it carries a message of balanced give-and-take. I advocate equal rights for all, through generative patterns of daily living that share the rewards of fertile friendship between all people and nations.

The Companion leads us into the complex world of personal, familial, communal, and global relationships. She instructs us in matters of mutuality and reciprocity. She presents us with opportunities to experience commitment and shared responsibility.

Handmaiden = Service

Mate / Wife = Equality

Sister / Friend = Loyalty

Companion Archetype

Faithfully toiling behind the scenes, serving the needs of her people, the Handmaiden is the unsung heroine of the world. Humility and loyalty are her strength and power. The Handmaiden crafts gifts of the heart, made with loving hands, given in gracious service, dedicated to the spirit of health and well-being for all. She works quietly without fanfare, finding her reward in the accomplishment of a task well done. Sadly, she is generally taken for granted by the outside world— which could not survive without her.

In this painting, she stands serene, yet purposeful, carrying her water jar to a sacred oasis in the dry mesa of her homeland. The azure vault of sky stretches forever above the boundless burnt-sienna badlands, where the Handmaiden carries the water and tends the hearth-fire for a thriving community. She walks a sagebrush-bordered trail with her familiar companion, Cat. Animals can always be found accompanying the Handmaiden on her rounds, lending moral and physical support to the woman at her tasks. She, in turn, gives loving consideration to her loyal pet's needs.

There is little adventure or drama in the life of a Handmaiden. She is no servant, but a keeper of the traditional ways, a caretaker of her community, painstakingly tending her daily routine and keeping her hearth secure. She is directly descended from the great hearth-keeper goddess of ancient days— Hestia— sister and quiet companion to all the Olympians. Another of her fore-mothers is Hagar, handmaid to Sarah, in the biblical tale.

Invocation to the Handmaiden:
Help me love the work I do and do the work I love.
Let me appreciate the beauty and pleasure of
simple tasks and shared joys in daily living.
Help me to allow others to serve me,
as I enjoy serving them.

I pray to protect my home and
keep all I love safe from harm.

MOON IN CANCER: Intuitive care-giving; Sentimental nurture; Timidity
TAROT: V = "HIEROPHANT" Ruled by tradition, Routine provides security

Handmaiden
with companion
by Karin Weiss 12/25/99

THE HANDMAIDEN

The Mate-Wife establishes, upholds, and champions the honor of family, ethnic, or community heritage. She is the Matriarch who holds the keys to the kingdom in her regal grasp, standing equal to her partner in status and power. Once having stepped over the marriage threshold, a woman is never again innocent— for she has been inside the sanctum and gleaned its deepest secret: in patriarchy, men gain stature when they can claim a wife.

In the painting, she sits in mindful meditation and holds sacred the memory of her ancestors. She is accompanied by her own equal companion, the cat, who mimics her contemplative gestures as it helps her conjure venerable forebears. She is the matriarch of her family and clan, given stewardship of its traditions and history. She may have children to whom she will bequeath the sacred heritage, but her primary role is as team-mate to her husband. The Mate-Wife is a mature woman, seasoned by experience, clear in her motives, unmoved by sentimental longings, and holding sovereignty of her own life.

Perhaps she is a modern incarnation of the Greek goddess, Hera, prototypical matriarch whose story foreshadows lives of famous women in our own times, such as Eleanor Roosevelt, Rose Kennedy, and Jacqueline Bouvoire Kennedy who, each in her own way, stoically withstood a partner's betrayals in order to uphold her own values of heritage, status, or honor. Such women have always been the unacknowledged power behind the success and fame of their high-ranking men.

Invocation to the Mate-Wife:
Help me honor my feminine heritage and claim equal power in my relationships. Let me build sovereignty of my life, without dominating others. Help me to believe in my capacity to bear fruitful ambitions and produce a bountiful progeny.

I pray to uphold the memory of my forebears with dignity and pride.

SUN IN CAPRICORN: Responsible; Pragmatic; Prestige-seeking; Domineering
TAROT: VI = "LOVERS" Interplay of opposites; Urge to merge; Equality

Guardian
of Family
Histories

—by Karla
Weiss

9/6/99 Labor
Day

THE MATE/WIFE

The Sister-Friend is the part of us who knows best how to listen. She helps us learn from our mistakes. As Sister-Friends enter each other's lives, they bring a new vision, a new hope for the future, a new sense of strength through womanly companionship.

In the painting, there are seven sisters— four humans and three dolphins— all sharing a magical moment of play under the watchful gaze of grandmother moon. In their enchanted bower, they stroke and groom each other in silent understanding of their ancient and primal bond. The dolphins come as teachers of the elemental power of female relations. The trees are without leaf, perhaps representing the barren aspect of female companionship, which suggests a different kind of creativity in which the progeny can be new ideas, visions, dreams of prosperity and healing for the world. Perhaps this gathering of sisters are bringing down the energy of the Plieades— the legendary constellation known as "the seven sisters" who are said to have transformed themselves in solidarity as protest against the crude and cruel treatment of women by the patriarchy.

Sister-Friends may meet in private, perhaps in secret, but surely always in confidentiality—keeping each other's counsel, sharing each other's joys and sorrows with the compassionate wisdom and intimate wit that is born only out of female bonding. It is for this reason that patriarchal institutions perpetually strive to silence women's movements and turn us against each other.

Invocation to the Sister / Friend:

Help me recognize and meet my sisters all over the earth.
Let us play together to heal each other.
Let us bond together to re-create an inclusive
and respectful worldwide community of peace.

I pray for women to support one another with fairness and honesty.

SUN IN AQUARIUS: Intuitive innovation; Non-conformist; Sagacious counsel
TAROT: VII = "CHARIOT" Take-charge attitude; Supportive guidance; Winner

THE SISTER-FRIEND

Challenge / Pursue / Dare

At Last Quarter Moon I am the fearless Warrior woman, fighting for the equal rights and defending the boundaries of your physical, emotional, mental and spiritual Being. Within every woman, I raise the banner of heroic self-expression. I carry the sword of justice and wield the spear of fair play. I am the Heroine, your armor against subjugation and persecution. I am the Huntress, your autonomous power to repel assault and hunt that which you need to survive and thrive. I am the Rebel within, whose anger enables you to break oppressive rules and take a stand for your own Truth.

Do you recall raising your rage against abuses and violations done to women, children and minorities? I am with you at those times, bolstering your cause. Do you recall a time when you dared to reveal yourself, despite the disapproval of those who would shame you? I was there, standing beside you and holding up your courage.

My moon-phase empowers you to break free from all restraints and take action toward your highest goals. It is a time to declare your rights and territory. I help all women take back the night, take home the victory, take in the lost, and take heart.

The Warrior is our inner champion who breaks the shackles that hold women captive in a man-ruled world. She brings courage, where before there was only fear. She brings proud self-confidence, where before we felt shame. Aflame with blazing passion, the Warrior within Woman wields an awesome erotic force that has potential to transform the world.

Heroine = Dedication

Huntress = Discipline

Rebel = Tenacity

Warrior Archetype

The Heroine initiates us into realms of higher mind, awakening our passion to impact the greater good, arousing our desire to achieve larger goals in life. She leads Woman's pursuit of knowledge and demands freedom for us to choose our own paths. The Heroine carries the Warrior's banner in the battle for women's truth and liberty. The fight waged by a Heroine is for women, everywhere, to recover their autonomy.

In the painting, four goddesses converge or convene. Perhaps they debate the fate of the failed patriarchy. Athena stands overseeing an anxious-looking Liberty, her disapproving eye on the tiny torch of freedom held aloft under her gaze. Athena, instead, offers a spear— sharp-stabbing and menacing— with a will to combat. Above them, the rainbow messenger goddess, Iris, flies in, holding a scroll that encourages dialogue and negotiation. Beneath them, a harried and blind-folded Justice scampers frantically, to bring in the balancing scales.

These four are specific figures from classic myth who have been co-opted into the dominator system to do much of the dirty-work of a corrupt legal and religious code. Hopefully, when these goddesses meet, they can unite their forces to re-align the rainbow-band of varied philosophies and life-views held by peoples around the globe into a cooperative, mutually respectful, new model for civilization. Maybe they will bring women into leadership.

Invocation to the Heroine:
Help me recognize my higher purpose
and dare to follow its un-trod path.
Let me express my truth without fear of
ridicule or rejection, so that my voice will be
heard by those who will heed it. Help me stay true to
my highest vision in the face of obstacles and opposition.

I pray for women to attain positions of
authority to wage peace and prosperity for all.

SUN IN SAGITTARIUS: Far-seeing; Expansive philosophy; Unique Genius
TAROT: VIII = "JUSTICE" Every action weighs out in Karmic balance

Guardians
of The Heroine
— Karin Weiss
11/20/98

HEROINE

The Huntress is the strategist of feminine campaigns for balance and power. She works both for women's survival in a male-dominated world, and for women's acquisition of territory, wealth, and position. Her skills require disciplined, practiced training; her actions must be carefully considered; her goals patiently pursued. The Huntress is a great adventurer, a daredevil, a risk-taker. Yet, she is purposeful, deliberate, resolved in her goals. Leaving little to chance, she bides her time, waits for the opportune moment to make her strike.

In the painting, a long-armed female Robin Hood aims her arrow off into the forest, while her two dogs stand poised to take chase. The Huntress must possess the courage and stomach to bring down another living creature when necessity demands. This is a prospect many women deny themselves, thinking it always cruel and wrong to kill. Yet, there are times when death is the kinder of available options, and at such times, the Warrior Huntress' arrows can bring relief from suffering, or attain safety from a menace.

This Huntress may be Artemis, protecting her sacred space and the sanctity of the goddess' privacy from encroaching intruders. She wears the pointed cap and short skirt with knee-high moccasins, attributed to legendary Amazon warriors of some ancient Libyan tribes. Dark-skinned, bare-breasted, and lightly armed— she is free to run through her sun-streaked wilderness at ease, blending into her surroundings, undetected.

Invocation to the Huntress:
Help me to aim my sights clearly
on my highest goal. Let my mental arrows
find their target, and my actions leave
their desired mark. Help me to discipline
myself toward superior achievements.

I pray for patience to await the propitious
moment to go after the goal I set.

MOON IN CAPRICORN: Pragmatic; Leads by mastery; Stealth
TAROT: XI = "STRENGTH" Tames by spiritual force; Disciplined mind.

THE HUNTRESS

The Rebel wields our Warrior's sword and carries the shield of woman-power. She raises the battle cry in women's war against the cruelties and injustices of society. She is motivated by a belief in the inalienable glory of her cause, and she sees herself a martyr to an ideal. The Rebel is a revolutionary, upsetting comfortable habits of tradition, breaking rigid rules of convention. Her presence within us can both terrify and reassure us.

In the painting, a wild red-haired Valkyrie-Amazon sits astride her fierce war-horse, menacing her enemies with her raging fury. Her horned headgear and sickle-bladed sword reflect the Crescent Moon, and her jeweled shield bears the sign of Venus, epitome of feminine powers. Perhaps she is a version of Valeda, the Celtic warrior priestess who was said to be so ferocious in her mystical powers that whole armies of Romans were stopped in their tracks and took route upon hearing her piercing war-cry, or sighting her wild-riding form at the head of her barbarian troops.

The woman who can equal men in ferocity and fighting is rare in modern "civil" times, yet she lurks in women's hearts and rages to be let free. She has recently been revived for us in the fictitious "Xena, Warrior Princess" television series of the 1990's.

Invocation to the Rebel:
Help me to use my anger productively
to create desired change. Whether I win or lose
the battle, help me to believe in my cause
and carry on with the work at hand.

I pray to increase my courage to
fight the just and right cause.

SUN IN ARIES: Aggressive; Spontaneous leader; Willful determination
TAROT: XVI = "TOWER" Upsets status quo; Chaotic change

THE REBEL

Sacrifice / Sanctify / Heal

At Balsamic Moon I am the inner Wise Woman, ultimate source of womanly power. I am the Mystic, delving spiritual roots of feminine wisdom. I am the Priestess, teaching goddess-knowledge to those who come to learn at my temple, which is found in the body and mind of every woman. I am the Witch-Shaman, instructing mysteries of life and death. Many fear my power, for it transcends rational thought.

I fly with the spirit-powers throughout the Cosmos. I am ever-present, every-place, and all-times. I am the ghosts of all the women sacrificed in the Burning Times of past, present and future, all over the globe. I haunt those who are guilty of persecution, and I empower those who survive, working to heal the world of such blights. Do you remember times when you felt connected to all Life? I am your guide to the Universe's wisdom, for I bring light to your inner consciousness.

My lunar phase is associated with dark mysteries of the unconscious, and I wait in the silent period of stillness that precedes another New Moon birth— at which I will preside as the Midwife.

With the Wise Woman, we travel to the Dark Queen's underworld— the spiritual womb where the coal of basic intellect transforms to become the diamond of true wisdom. The ego dies, to be reborn as a newly creative power. All are gathered in the Wise Woman's embrace. But in our human blindness and deafness, we arrogantly disregard her single all-important lesson: We are all One.

Mystic = Meditation

Priestess = Reverence

Witch-Shaman = Transformation

Wise Woman Archetype

71

The Mystic is the keeper of our inner temple, presiding over the realm of meditation, prayer, serene solitude, prophecy, and lucid dreaming— all solitary psychic mysteries perused in the privacy of our hearts. The Mystic within speaks only in whispers, if she speaks at all— yet, her word carries great power in our lives. The Mystic within communes with the angels, her oracles, her god/dess, and her inner selves. She is content to do no more than contemplate what she has heard or seen, for she dwells in mystery, seeing all sides of every matter from within her own duality.

In the painting, the horizon is aglow in either a setting or rising sun, while the Mystic's moon-blessed magic sends forth an opalescent stream of dream-wisdom. A tiny owl hoots her regenerative call, and a shimmering snake winds around the magenta trees of a sacred grove, announcing the prospect of perpetual life within cycles of transformational change. The dual-bodied Mystic holds a sword to cut away outworn ideas from the shadowed past, and a grail to serve up the nectar of renewed life. This may be a female Janus, or a human version of the two-faced Egyptian sphinx, Akeru, who guarded the gates of sunset and sunrise— standing between yesterday and tomorrow. The Mystic shows us that we are all both alive and dead, everything both a lie and true. Nothing is all or none. Life is bathed in the dream's ethereal certainty, ever caught between moments of time.

Invocation to the Mystic:

Help me to keep my faith in miracles, and let me
stand as witness to the truth of feminine mysteries.
Let women's prayers be fulfilled, that where evil
exists, good will flood its place.

I pray to connect with my own guiding spirits.

SUN IN PISCES: Serene psychic; Imaginative dreamer; Escape to fantasy
TAROT: IX = "CRONE" Witness to secrets of the Universe; Humble wisdom

THE MYSTIC

The Priestess performs the rites and liturgies that give sacred meaning to our lives. She presides at the rituals that bring us power, preservation, or peace. She is our instructress in sacred knowledge, teaching the most ancient wisdom of the goddess. The Priestess teaches the tremendous power contained in symbol. She encourages us to re-create our own forms of sacrament, urges us to establish newfound rituals for worship.

In the painting, she holds her frame drum high, drumming the ancient rhythms of earth-based and goddess-blessed rituals, and dances to the heart-beat of all Creation. This modern-day priestess wears her head-band adorned with hawk feathers, perhaps donated by the young hawk, coming to perch near her now, and join in the ceremony.

In the mountain valley, a group of women gather around a bonfire to honor the earth and do rituals for peace. They appear childlike, diminutive, elfin— for the women are dwarfed in the majesty of the mountains surrounding them. It is a clear summer day, fresh water flows through the stream, and alpine flowers bloom at the Priestess' feet. Perhaps her dance is one of initiation to honor the blood-mysteries and woman-cycles of the young women coming of age. This dancing Priestess may be a modern-day Diana, or the descendant of native Medicine Women, drumming to honor all our relations.

Invocation to the Priestess:
Help me to conduct the rituals of my daily life
with reverence and serene dedication.
Let me feel the compassion of the goddess for
all creatures with whom I share my world.
Help me make, willingly, the sacrifices
needed to serve my highest purpose.

I pray to utilize my unique source of
power for the sake of all-peace.

MOON IN VIRGO: Discriminating; Practical knowledge; Exacting skills
TAROT: II = "HIGH PRIESTESS" Receptive wisdom; Balance of power

by Karin Weiss
"The Priestess Now"
10/98

THE PRIESTESS

The Witch-Shaman is shape-changer of our soul, the keeper of mystery and the maker of magic, who knows Nature's tongue and speaks with all creatures. She welcomes the seasons, praises the moon's monthly phases, and rejoices to see the evolving patterns of the Universe reflected in earth's mirror. The Witch-Shaman, casts the circle of wholeness and connectedness to the Universe. She works Magic, using ancient methods of calling on the higher powers of love for guidance, and conjures alternative realities from which we may choose and create our own destiny.

In the painting, she has taken the shape of the World Tree— delving to the depths of the earth through roots as ancient as time, and reaching to the heights of the heavens with branches as full as forever. She has entered the spirit of the trees in fall, when leaves are turning a burning-bush red. Behind her, the river waters flow cold azure, and the foothills on the distant shore are bathed in a patchwork of autumnal brilliance. Her arm-branches are entwined by a wisdom-snake, while from afar fly ravens to alight therein. The red-eyed wolf stands guard, but wary of the even fiercer flame-red tabby at the tree-goddess' feet. Perhaps she is the ancient Lady of Beasts. All animals are her "familiars" in that they are her blood-kin through the great Mother of all. The Witch-Shaman is sworn to protect them and honor all life, to let each be as they are created, and do harm to none.

Invocation to the Witch-Shaman:

Help me to reach into my deepest power to access my profound erotic remembrance, and celebrate life-everlasting. Let me join with my sisters in magic, to bless the earth and all who dwell here-in.

I pray to grow love and blessings, while detaching myself from need.

SUN IN SCORPIO: Deep knowledge held with passion; Secrets held in power
TAROT: I = "MAGICIAN" Creative willpower; Guardian at the crossroads.